Tell Me WHY

BUILDINGS
Questions and Answers

by
Rebecca Phillips-Bartlett

BEARPORT
PUBLISHING

Minneapolis, Minnesota

Credits

All images are courtesy of Shutterstock.com, unless otherwise specified. With thanks to Getty Images, Thinkstock Photo, and iStockphoto.

Cover – BNP Design Studio, Guz Anna, Taty Vovchek. 5 – Freder, nerthuz. 6–7 – GoodStudio, MediaProduction. 8–9 – Emil Timplaru, Magicleaf, jorisvo. 10–11 – LynxVector, Alexander Ryabintsev, Marti Bug Catcher. 12–13 – AndreaAstes, IUROVSKAIA EKATERINA, AIWD, Macrovector. 14–15 – GoodStudio, 4H4 Photography. 16–17 – frantic00, Javvani, Serg001, Amanita Silvicora. 18–19 – Javvani, DKDesignz, TZIDO SUN. 20–21 – antal, marcin jucha. 22–23 – Beboy_ltd, narak0rn, GoodStudio.

Bearport Publishing Company Product Development Team

President: Jen Jenson; Director of Product Development: Spencer Brinker; Managing Editor: Allison Juda; Associate Editor: Naomi Reich; Associate Editor: Tiana Tran; Art Director: Colin O'Dea; Designer: Elena Klinkner; Designer: Kayla Eggert; Product Development Assistant: Owen Hamlin

Library of Congress Cataloging-in-Publication Data is available at www.loc.gov or upon request from the publisher.

ISBN: 979-8-88916-394-7 (hardcover)
ISBN: 979-8-88916-399-2 (paperback)
ISBN: 979-8-88916-403-6 (ebook)

© 2024 BookLife Publishing
This edition is published by arrangement with BookLife Publishing.

North American adaptations © 2024 Bearport Publishing Company. All rights reserved. No part of this publication may be reproduced in whole or in part, stored in any retrieval system, or transmitted in any form or by any means, electronic, mechanical, photocopying, recording, or otherwise, without written permission from the publisher.

For more information, write to Bearport Publishing, 5357 Penn Avenue South, Minneapolis, MN 55419.

Contents

Tell Me Why 4

Why Are So Many Buildings Made of Bricks? 6

Why Did People Build Pyramids? 8

Why Do Many Religious Spaces Have
Stained Glass Windows? 9

Why Does Europe Have So Many Castles? 10

Why Do Castles Have Moats? 11

Why Is the White House White? 12

Why Is Big Ben Called Big Ben? 13

Why Do We Have Windmills? 14

Why Are Wind Turbines Different From Windmills? 15

Why Do Some Ancient Buildings Have Columns? 16

Why Do Lighthouses Have Lights? 17

Why Does the Leaning Tower of Pisa Lean? 18

Why Is the Statue of Liberty Green? 19

Why Do Bungalows Have One Floor? 20

Why Do Some Buildings Have Solar Panels? 21

Asking Questions 22

Glossary 24

Index 24

TELL ME WHY

Our world is full of amazing buildings. Whether new or old, they all have a story to tell. Buildings can teach us about different places and people around the world.

QUESTION
What questions do you have about buildings?

Buildings are made for all sorts of purposes. Some are meant for people to live in, some are art, and others are built to do certain jobs. All these different structures might make you wonder **WHY?**

WHY ARE SO MANY BUILDINGS MADE OF BRICKS?

People have been making buildings out of bricks for thousands of years. Bricks are very strong and unlikely to break. So, you don't need to do as much to take care of them.

Although they are strong, bricks are not perfect for all kinds of buildings. Sometimes, we build with wood, metal, or concrete. These **materials** let us make things in different ways.

WHY DID PEOPLE BUILD PYRAMIDS?

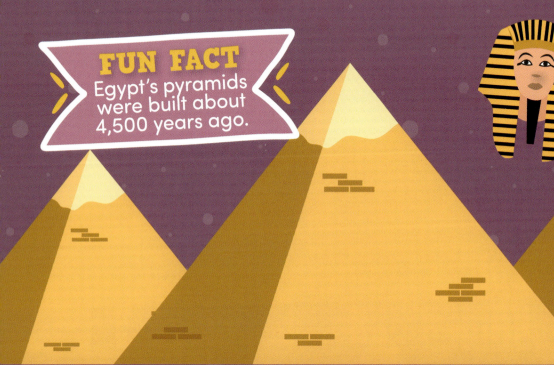

FUN FACT
Egypt's pyramids were built about 4,500 years ago.

Ancient Egyptians believed their rulers, the **pharaohs**, were living gods. They often built pyramids as tombs for the pharaohs. The huge size of the pyramids showed how important pharaohs were.

WHY DO MANY RELIGIOUS SPACES HAVE STAINED GLASS WINDOWS?

Many places of worship are filled with **symbols**. Some have stained glass windows that show important images and stories. The beautiful windows allow people to learn about the religion without having to read.

WHY DOES EUROPE HAVE SO MANY CASTLES?

FUN FACT
Germany has the most castles of any country in Europe.

Europe has more castles than any other **continent**. These structures became popular during the Middle Ages. At that time, powerful people ruled over the groups of people who lived on their land. They built castles to protect themselves and their land from attacks.

WHY DO CASTLES HAVE MOATS?

In the past, castles were often attacked by people who wanted to steal what was inside. **Moats** kept unwanted people out. These deep, water-filled ditches surrounded castles and helped stop thieves.

WHY IS THE WHITE HOUSE WHITE?

The president lives and works in the White House. When it was built, this building was painted in whitewash to protect the stone from cracking in freezing weather. This protection made the building stand out. People started calling it the White House.

WHY IS BIG BEN CALLED BIG BEN?

Big Ben is the nickname for a bell in a big clock tower in London, England. Some people believe it's named after Sir Benjamin Hall, who was in charge of having the bell put in the tower. Others think it's named after the boxer Benjamin Caunt, whose nickname was Big Ben.

QUESTION
Which story about Big Ben's name do you think is true?

WHY DO WE HAVE WINDMILLS?

Windmills are powered by nature. The buildings' large blades spin in the wind, and then machines inside work to grind grain into flour. Windmills can also be used to pump water or even make electricity.

FUN FACT

The first windmills were built in Asia more than 1,000 years ago.

WHY ARE WIND TURBINES DIFFERENT FROM WINDMILLS?

Today, there are more wind **turbines** than windmills. Although both are powered by wind, turbines are built to make electricity rather than do another job. The two structures look different, too. Wind turbines are much taller and have thinner blades.

Blades

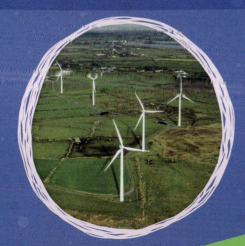

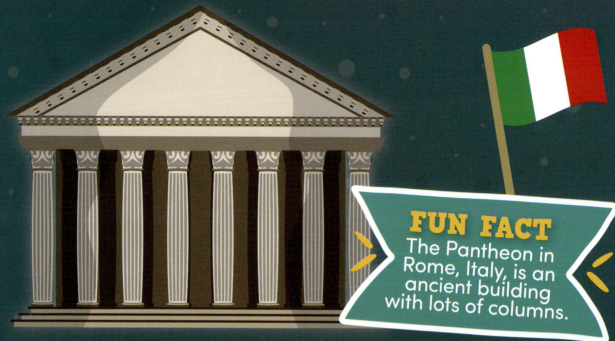

FUN FACT
The Pantheon in Rome, Italy, is an ancient building with lots of columns.

WHY DO SOME ANCIENT BUILDINGS HAVE COLUMNS?

Columns are tall pillars that help hold up the weight of big buildings. Structures with columns often last longer than those without. Sometimes, columns are added to buildings as decoration.

WHY DO LIGHTHOUSES HAVE LIGHTS?

Lighthouses are usually found along a coast close to the water. When sailors see the buildings' lights, they know land is near. They can use the light to safely guide their ships.

FUN FACT

The United States has more than 700 lighthouses. That's the most of any country!

17

WHY DOES THE LEANING TOWER OF PISA LEAN?

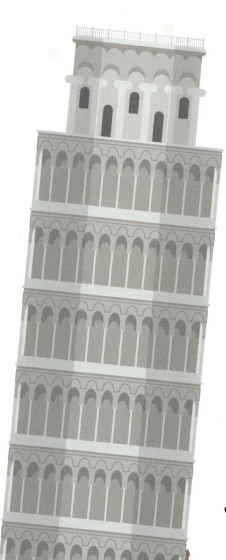

Italy's Leaning Tower of Pisa was supposed to be straight. However, the ground it was built on was too soft to hold the building's weight. The tower started leaning before it was even finished!

FUN FACT
People have tried to fix the tower's lean, but nothing has worked so far.

18

WHY IS THE STATUE OF LIBERTY GREEN?

The Statue of Liberty was made of a brown metal called copper. The metal sat out in open air, which contains **oxygen**. Over time, oxygen turns copper green.

WHY DO BUNGALOWS HAVE ONE FLOOR?

Bungalows were first built in south Asia. These buildings are often found in places with hot summers. These single-story buildings are easier to keep cool because hot air travels upward.

WHY DO SOME BUILDINGS HAVE SOLAR PANELS?

Solar panels collect **energy** from the sun and turn it into electricity. The sun is a **renewable** energy source, which means it won't run out. In addition to being renewable, it's better for Earth than other types of energy.

FUN FACT
Lots of solar panels near one another form what is called a solar farm.

Asking Questions

Buildings are everywhere. Often, we don't think twice about them. But if we do pay attention, we might start to have some questions.

Asking questions is a great way to learn about the world around you. There are so many interesting buildings to explore on Earth. So, stay curious, and keep asking questions!

QUESTION
What other questions do you have about buildings?

23

Glossary

columns strong poles that support the weight of a structure

continent one of Earth's seven large land masses

energy power that can make something work

materials things that can be used to make something else

moats deep ditches dug around castles and usually filled with water

oxygen a gas found in the air

pharaohs ancient Egyptian rulers

renewable able to be replaced by a natural process in a short period of time

symbols things that stand for something else

turbines machines that can be turned to create energy

Index

bell 13
blades 14–15
bricks 6–7
bungalows 20
castles 10–11
columns 16
copper 19
electricity 14–15, 21
lighthouses 17
pyramids 8
stained glass 9
tower 13, 18